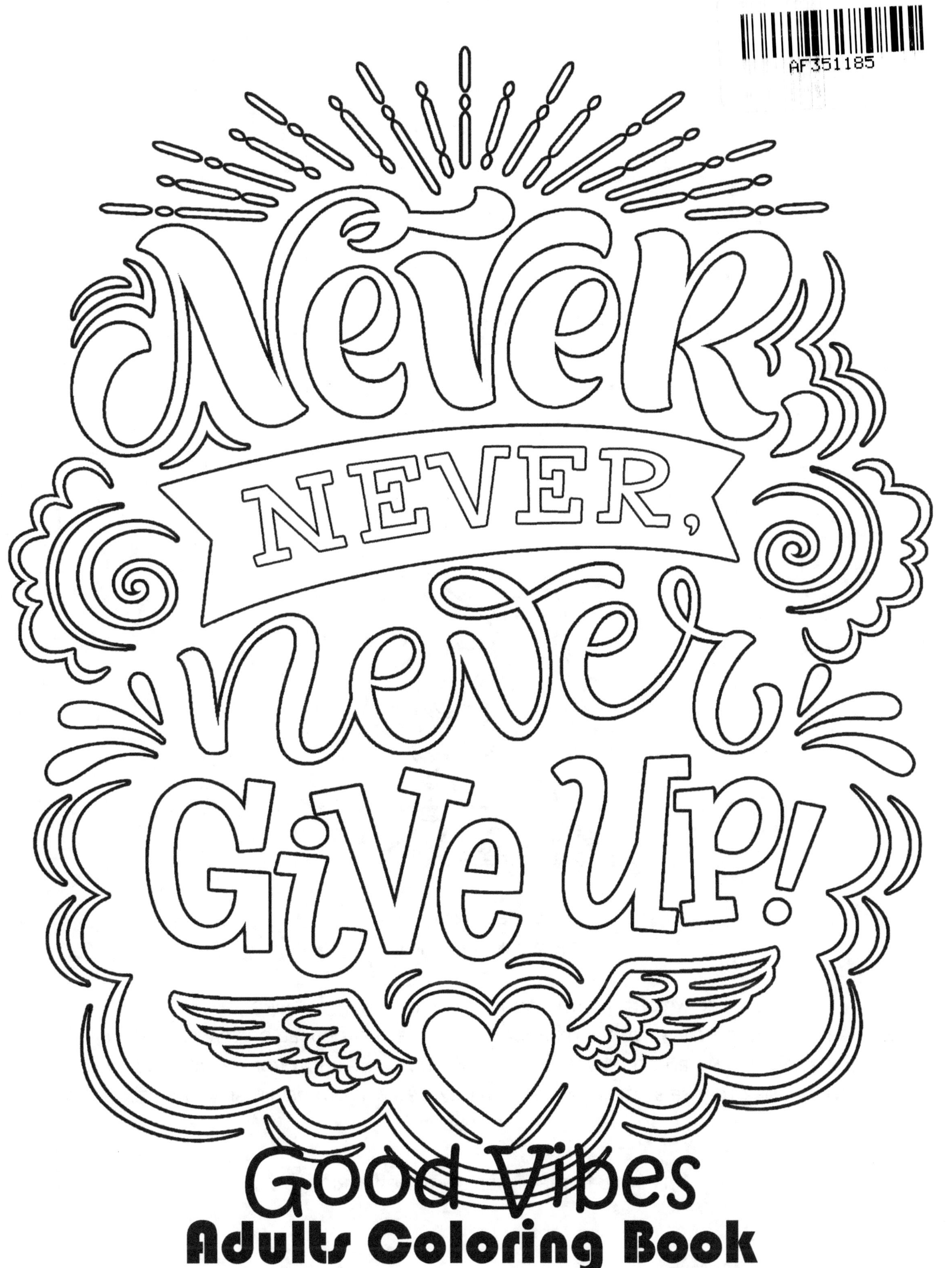

Never
NEVER,
never
Give Up!
Good Vibes
Adults Coloring Book

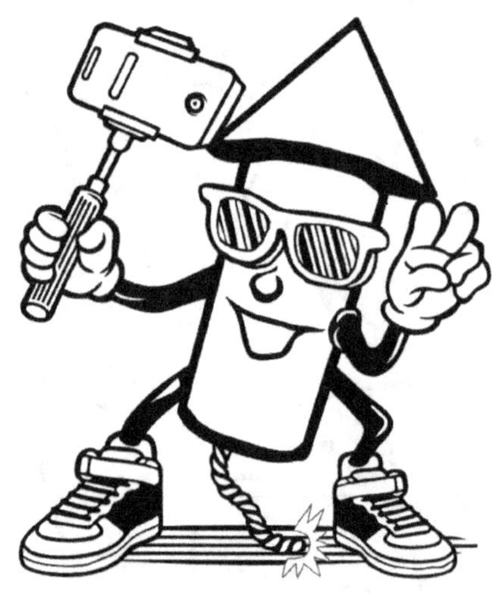

PUBLISHED IN 2020 BY

FIREWORK PUBLISHING

PRINTED IN THE UNITED STATE OF AMERICA

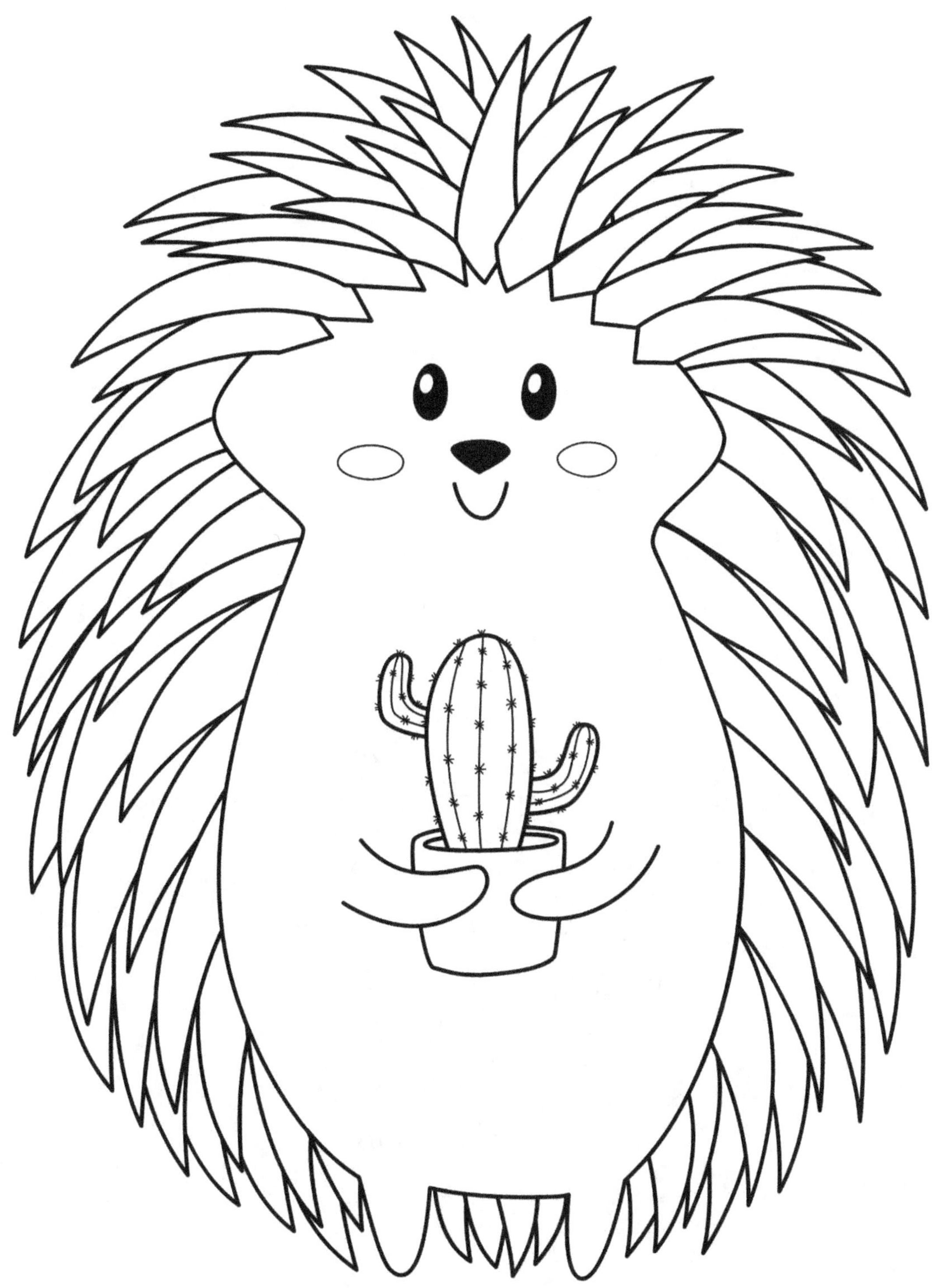

This book
belongs to

____

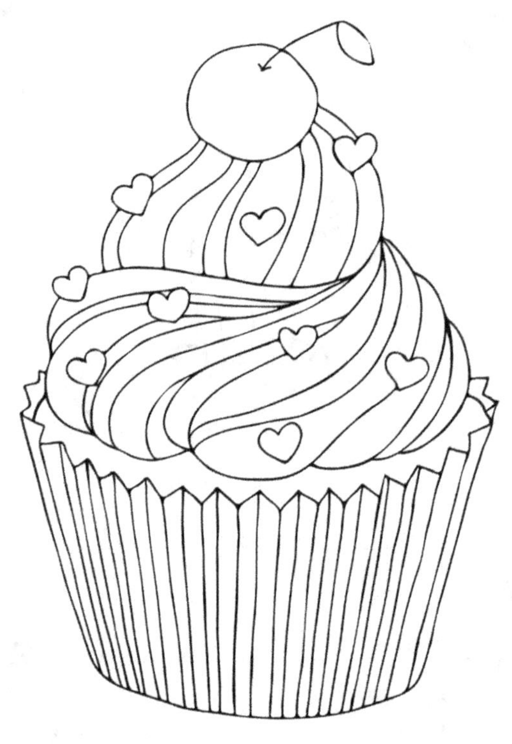

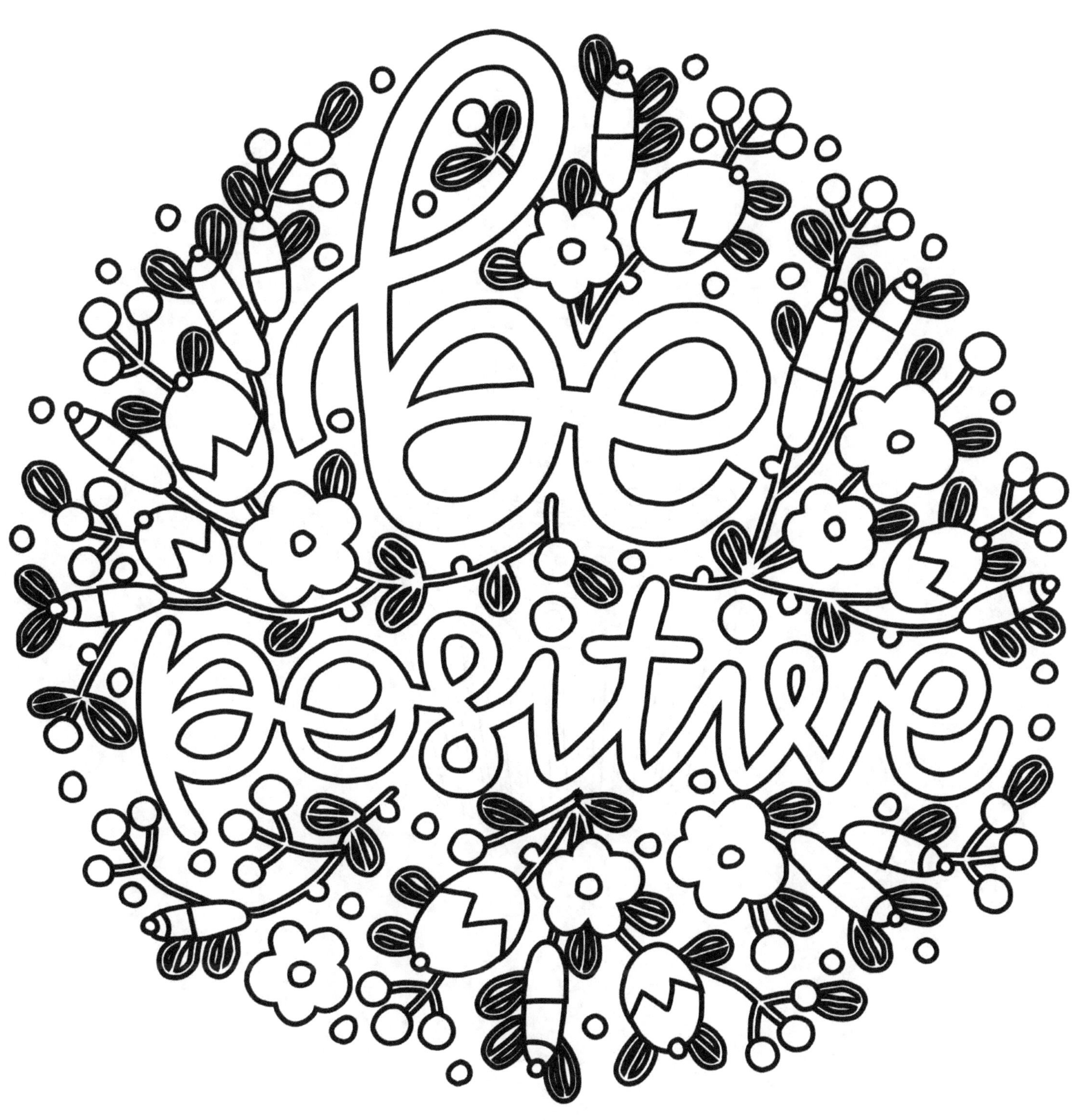

be
positive

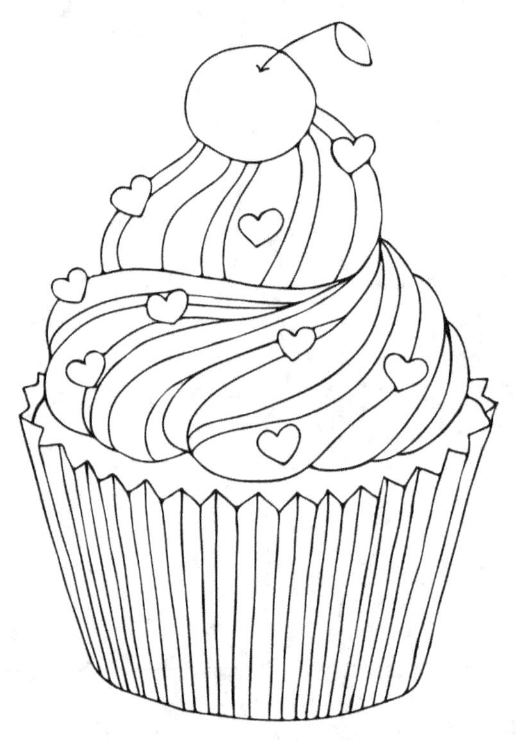

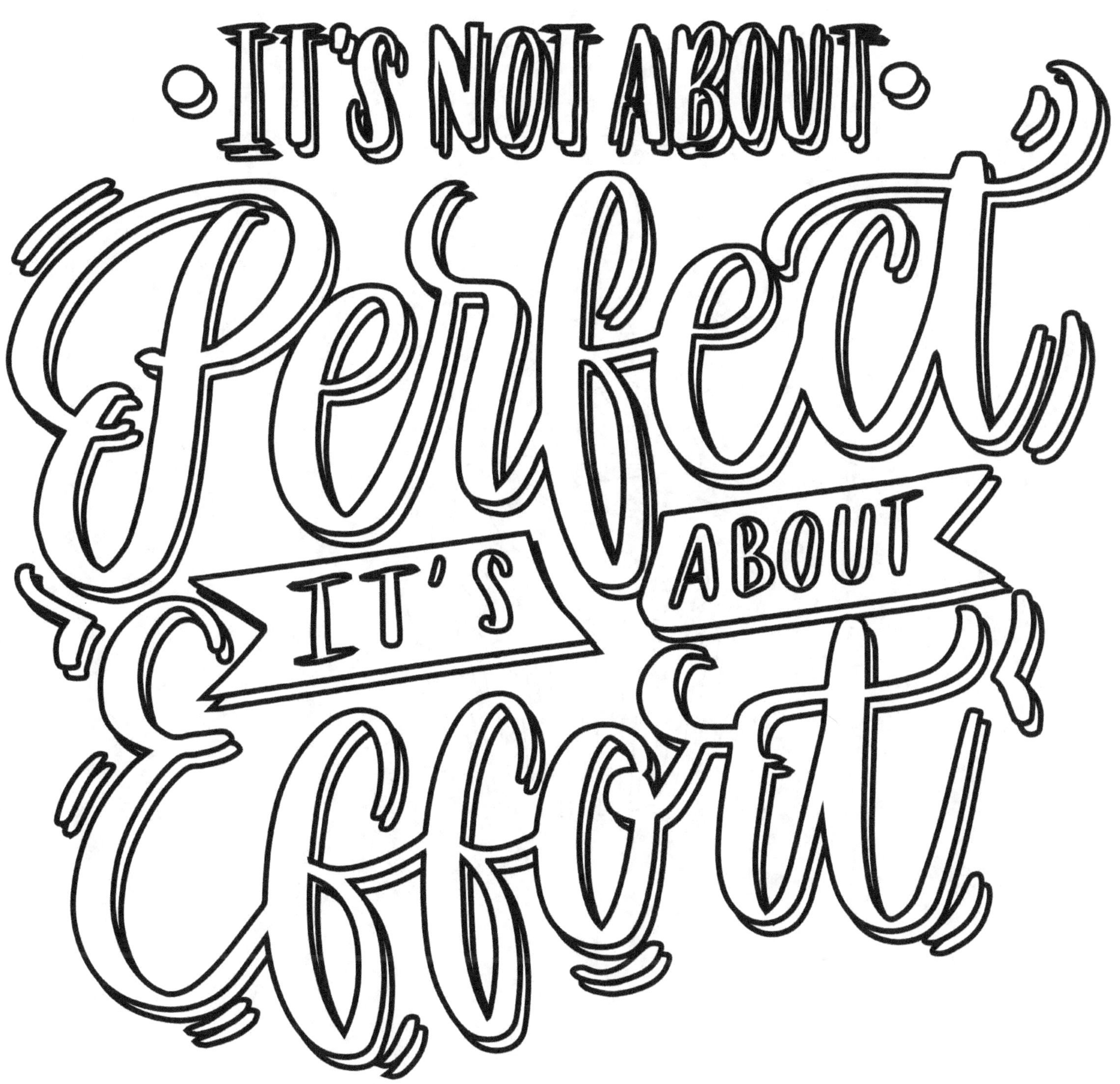
IT'S NOT ABOUT
Perfect
IT'S ABOUT
Effort

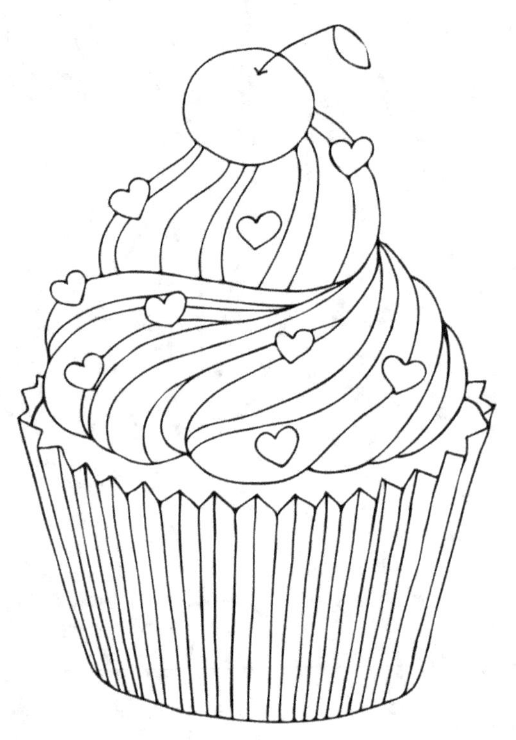

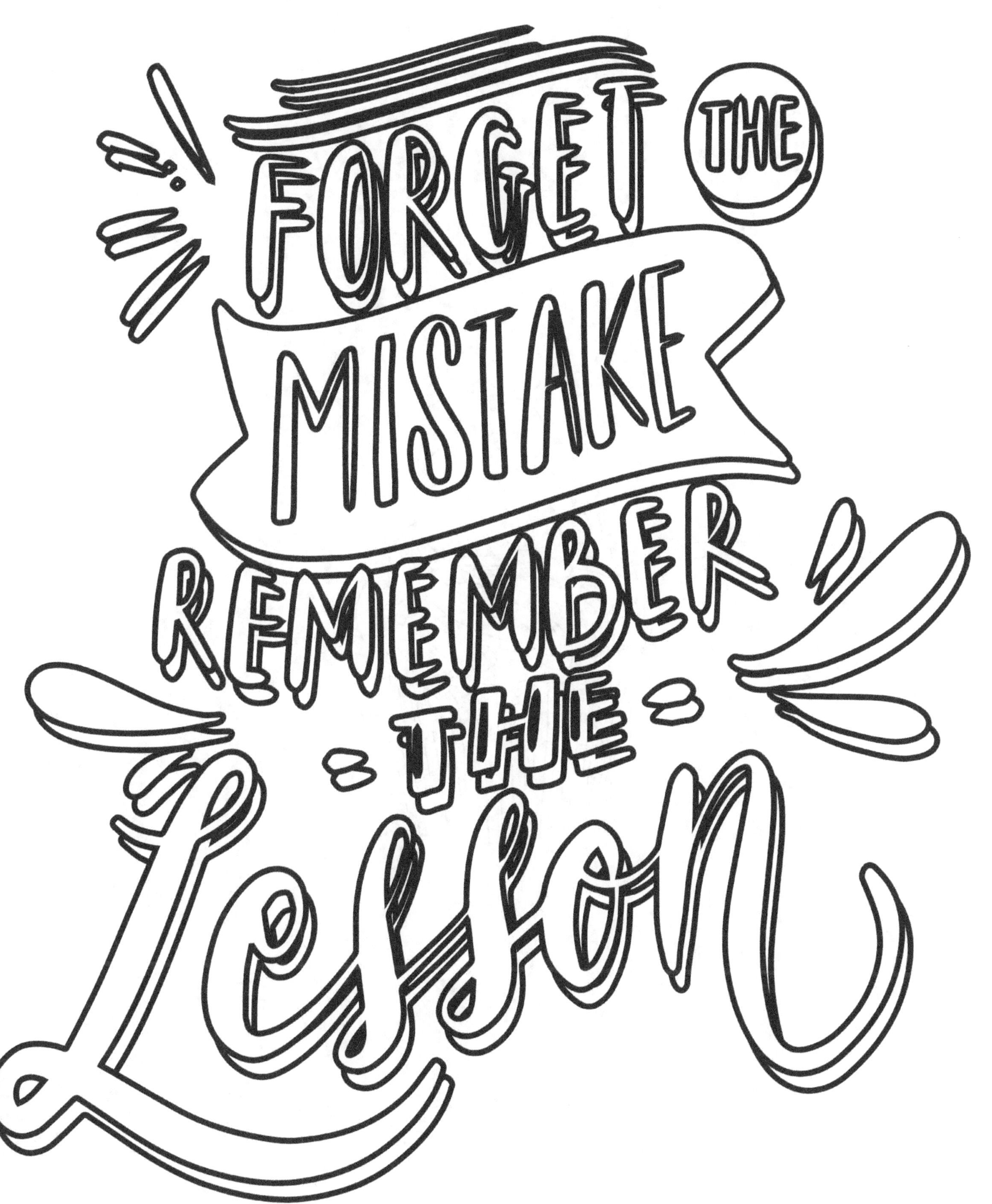

FORGET THE
MISTAKE
REMEMBER
THE
Lesson

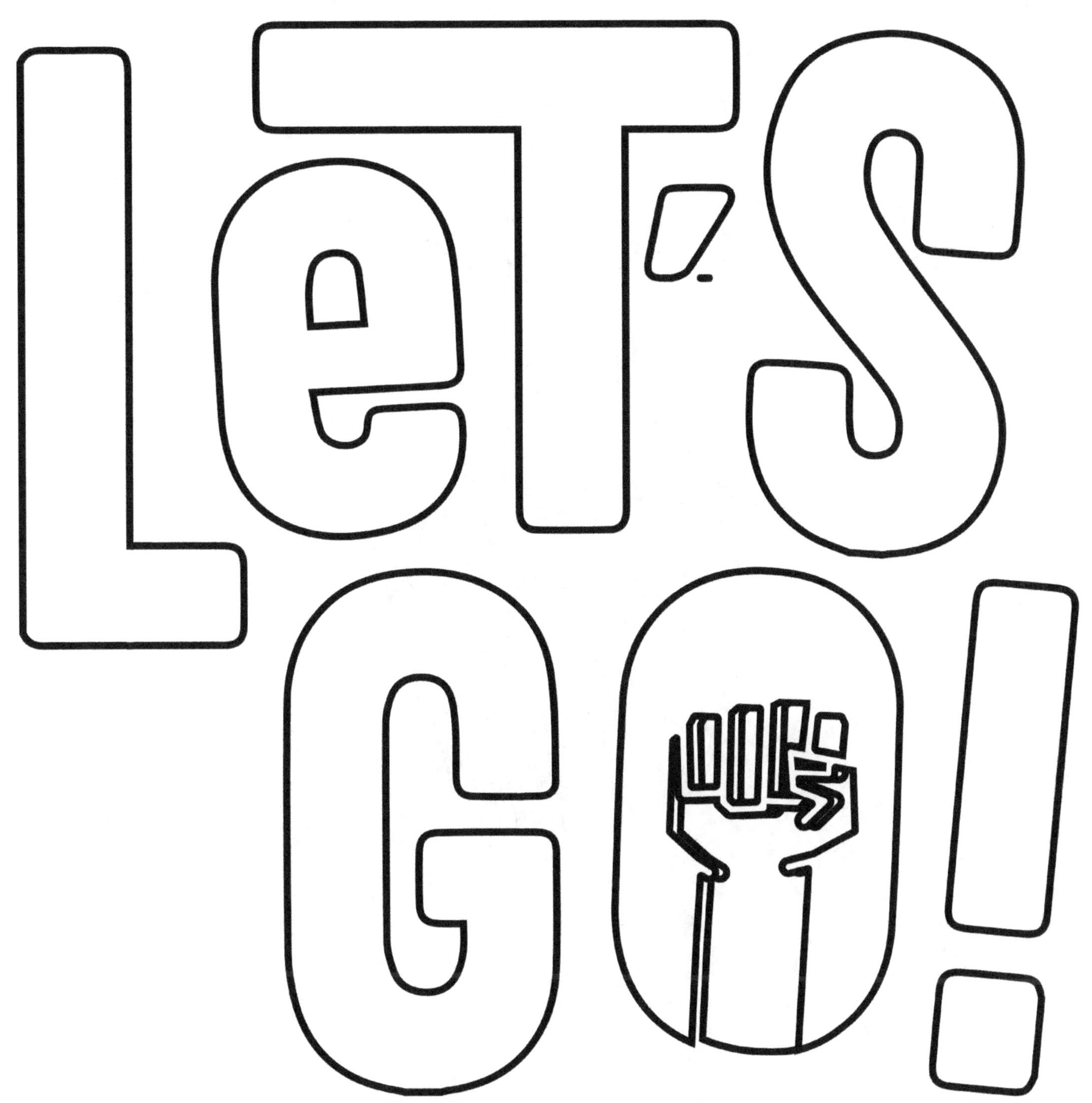
LET'S
GO!

It's cool to be kind

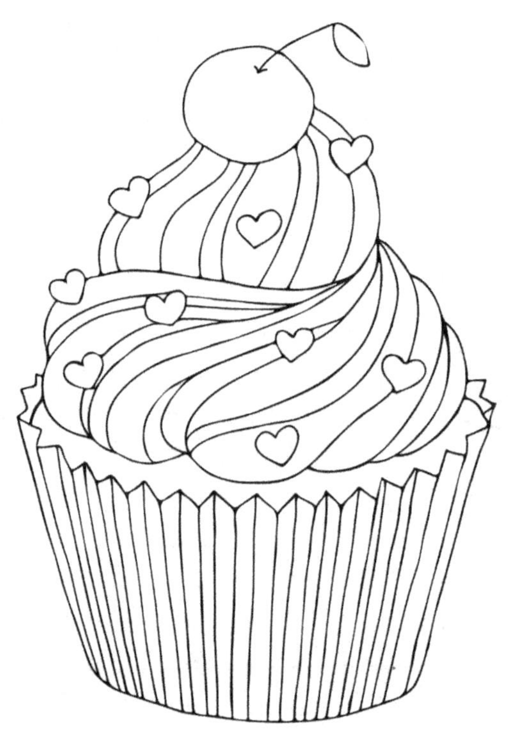

big
dream
big
act

Stay
POSITIVE
&
GOOD THINGS
Will
Happen

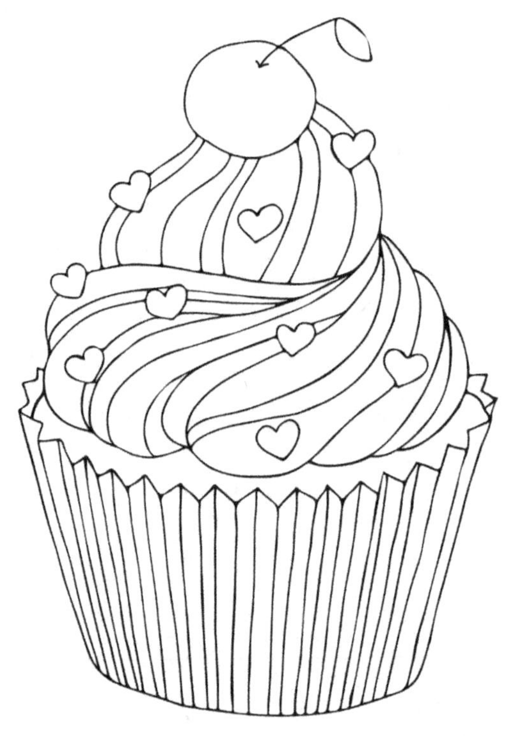

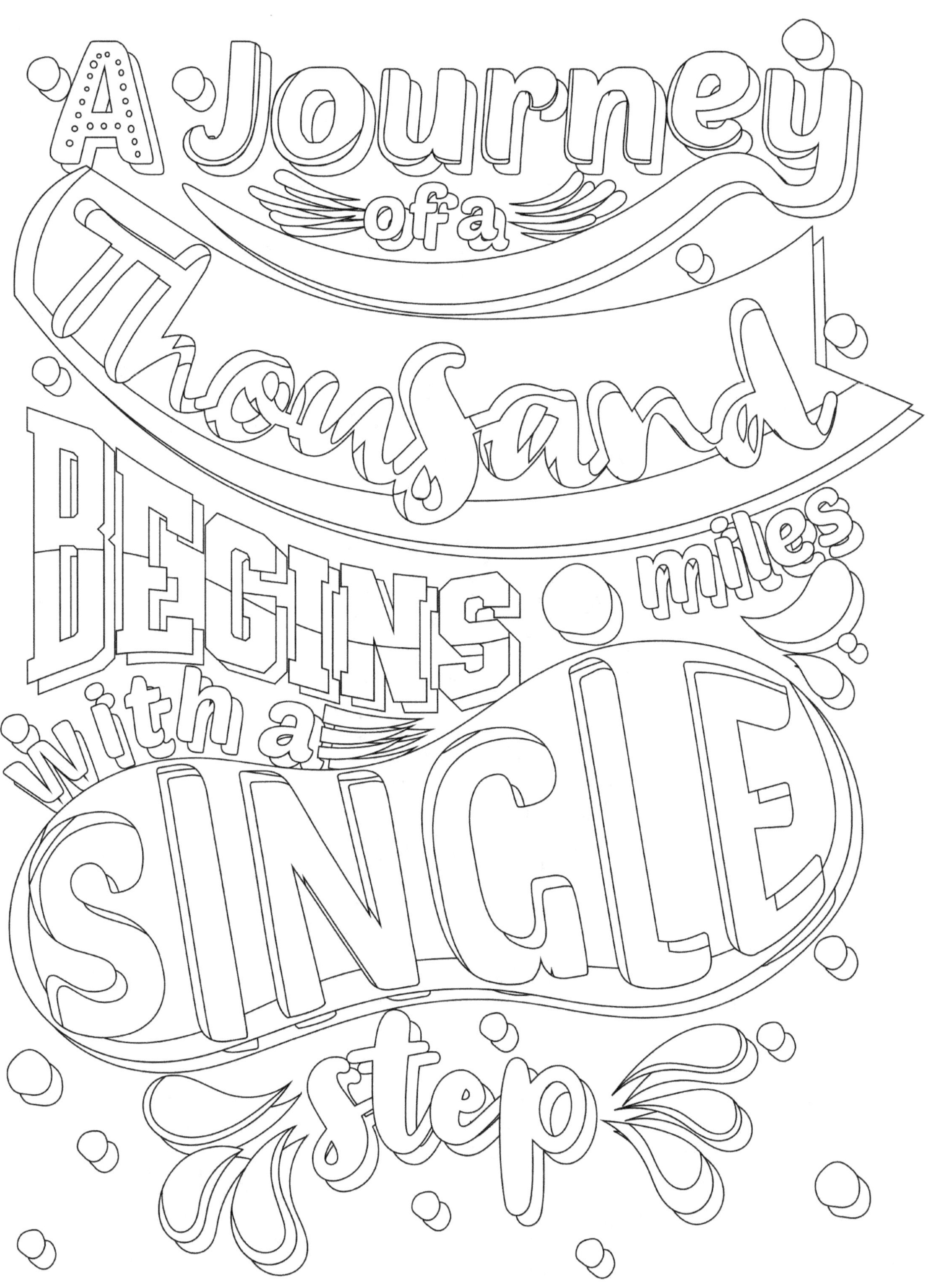

A Journey
of a
Thousand
BEGINS miles
with a
SINGLE
step

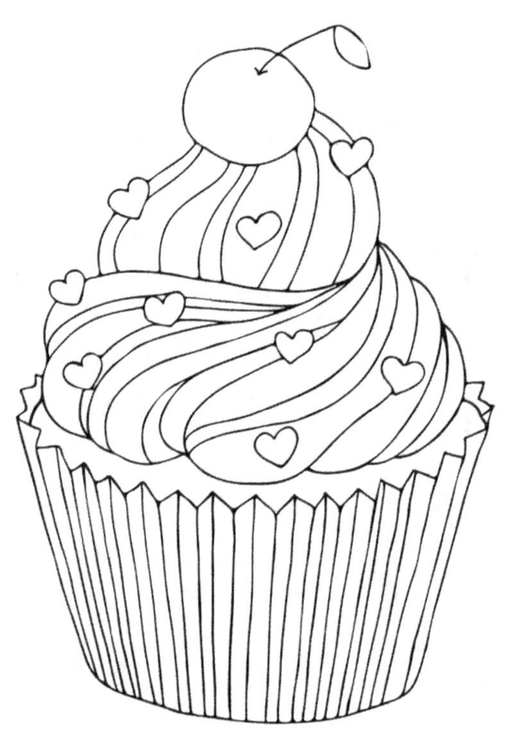

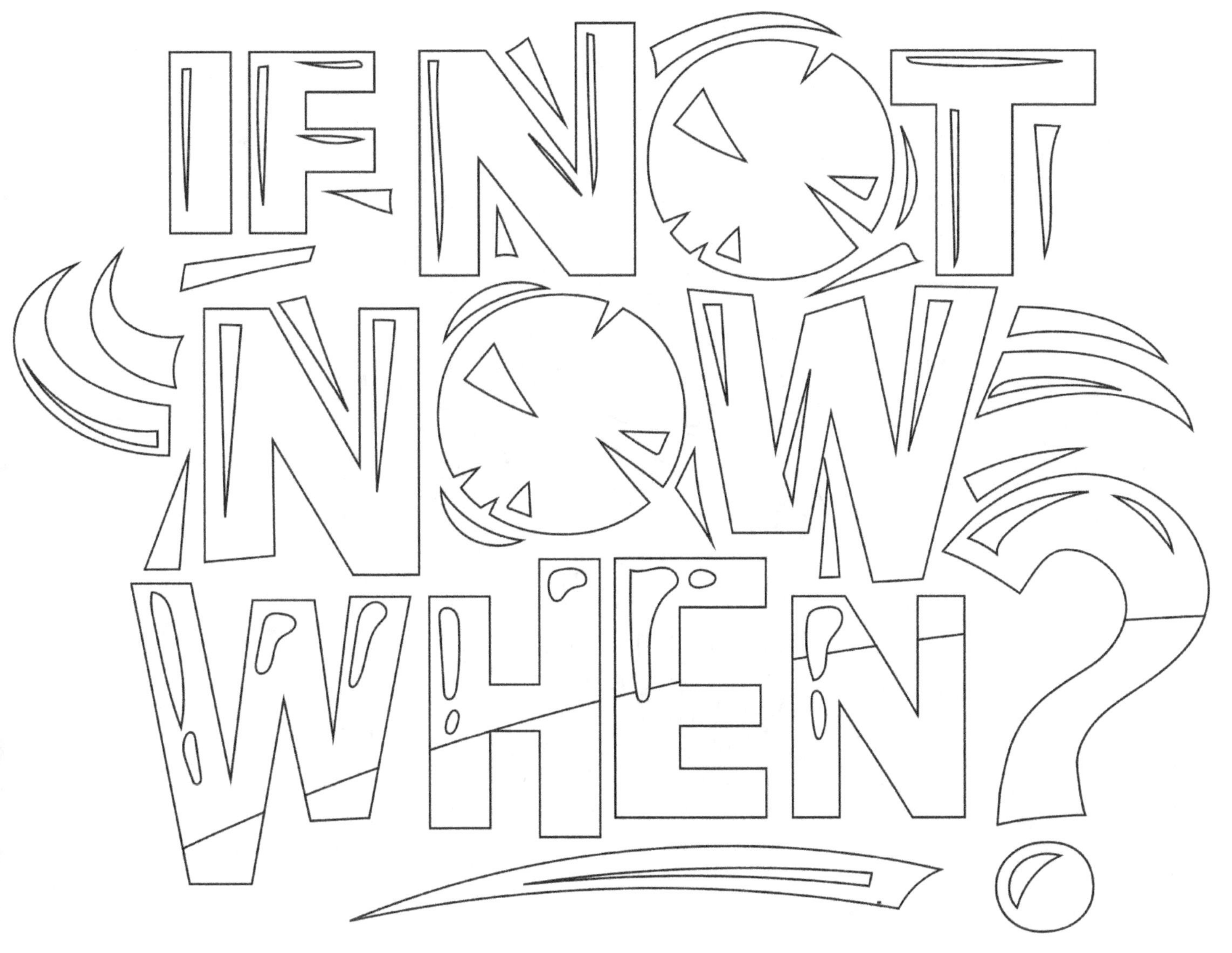
IF NOT
NOW
WHEN?

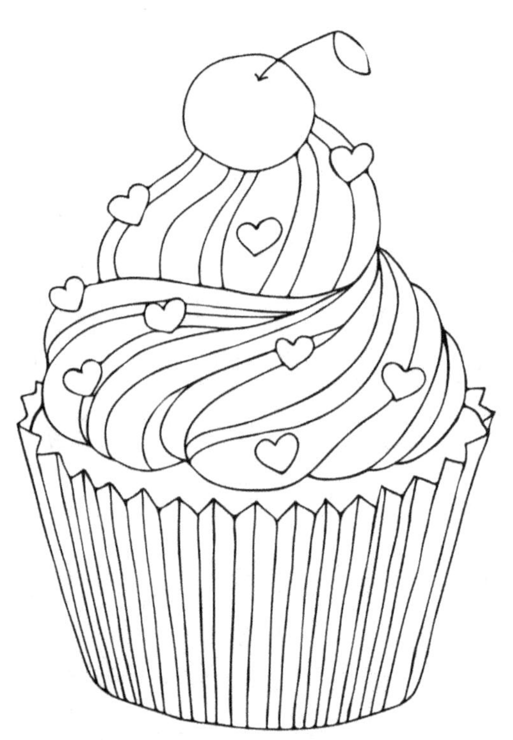

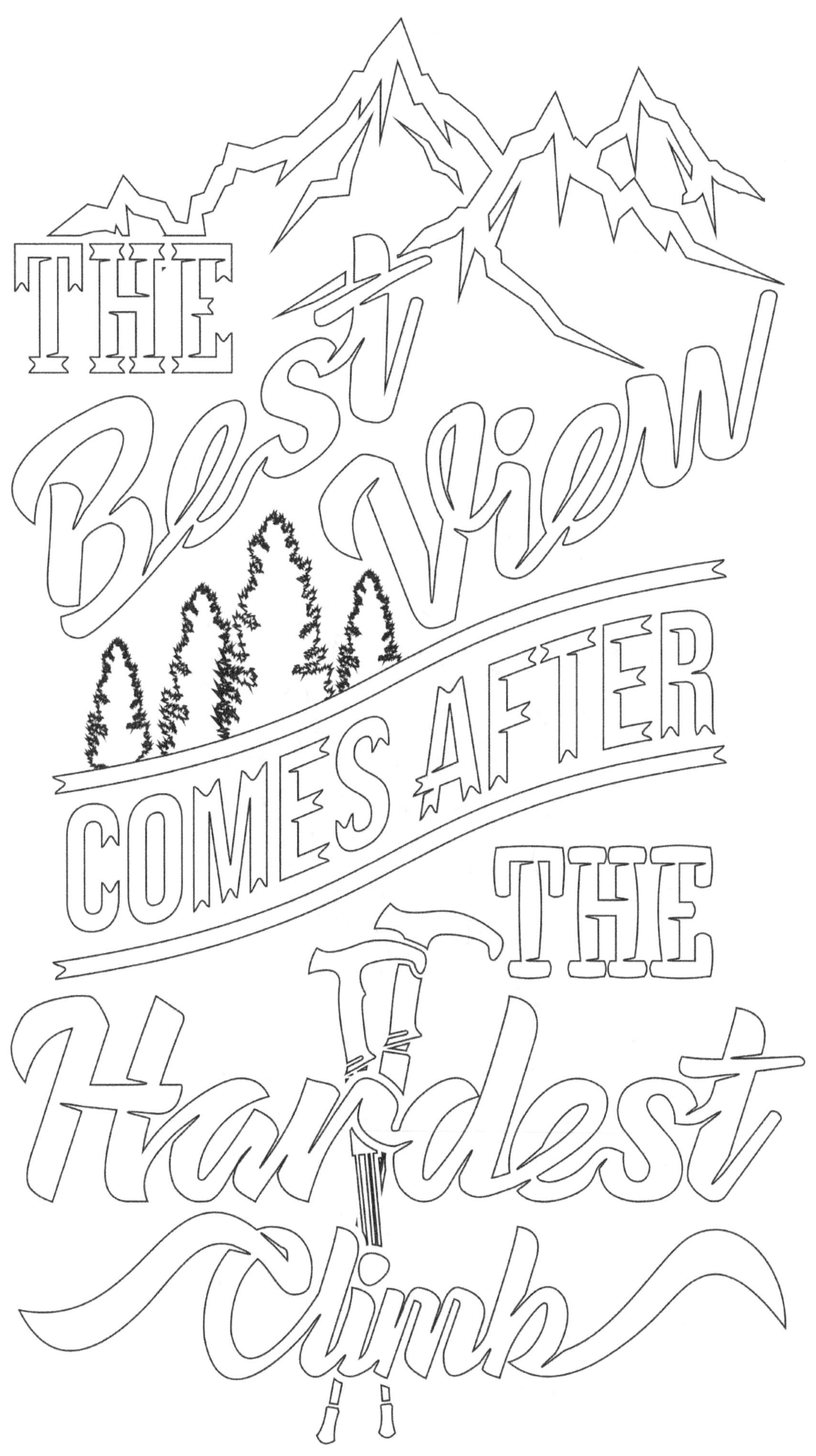

THE
Best View
comes AFTER
THE
Hardest
Climb

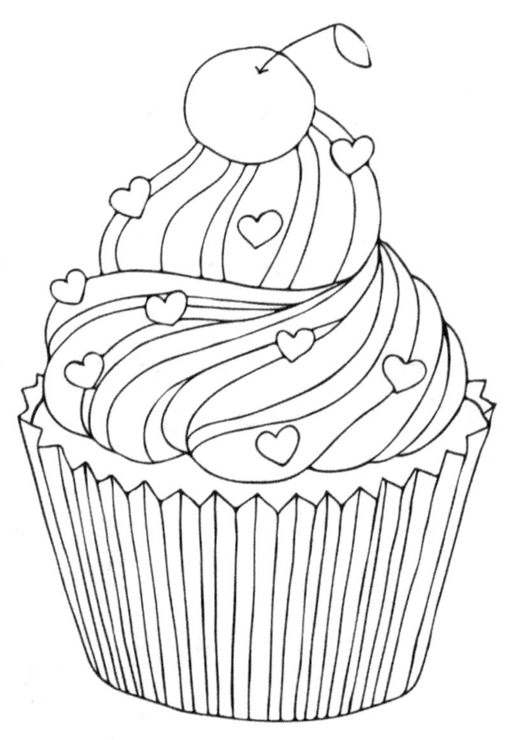

WORK
HARD IN
SILENCE
LET YOUR
SUCCESS
BE YOUR
NOISE

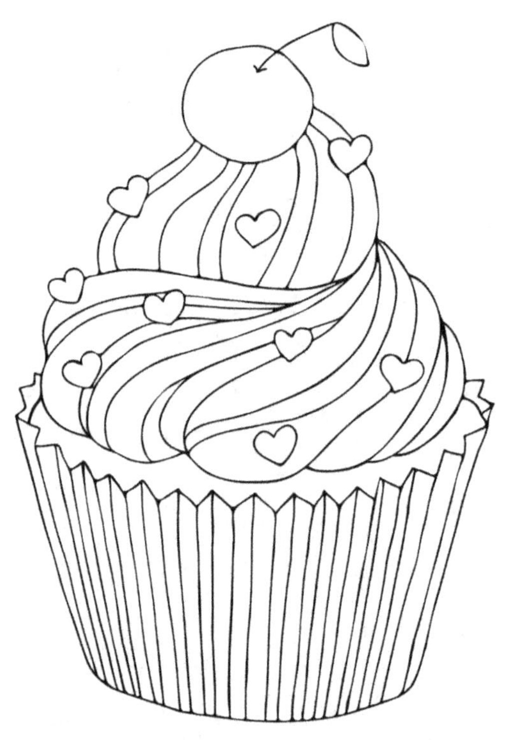

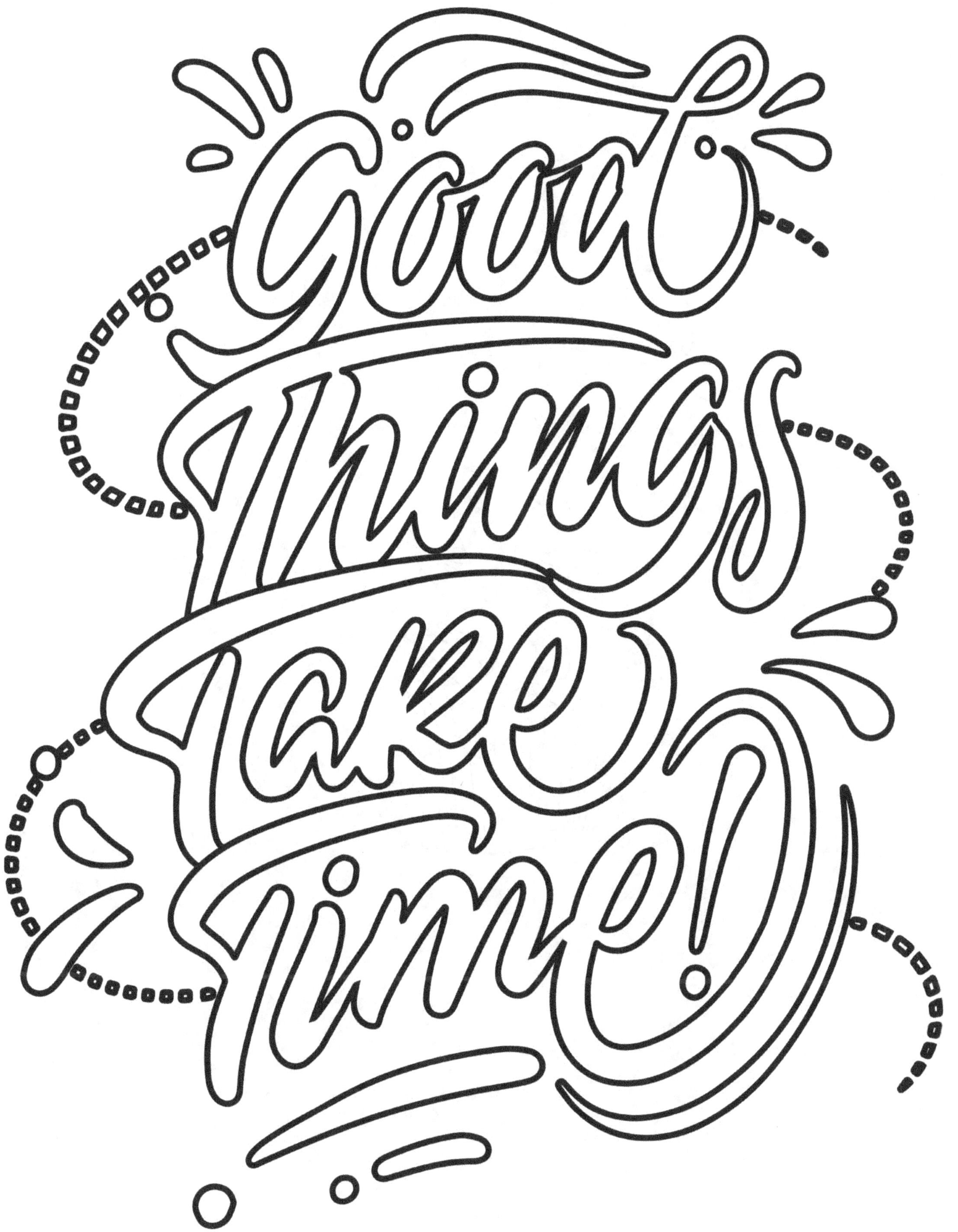
Good
Things
Take
Time!

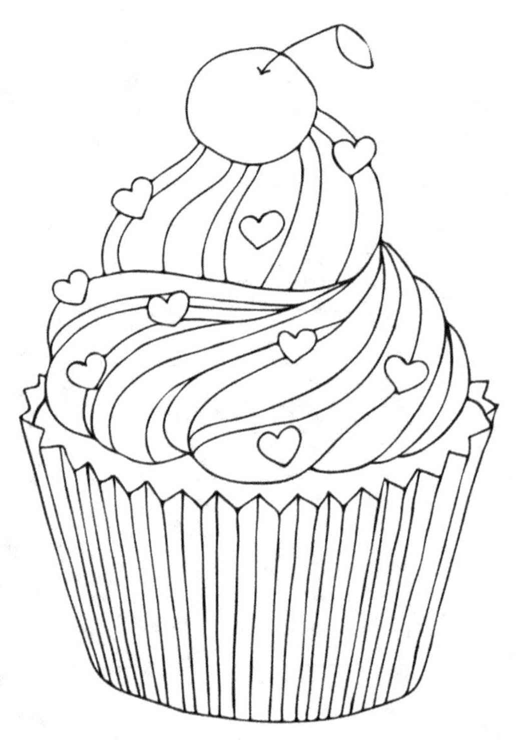

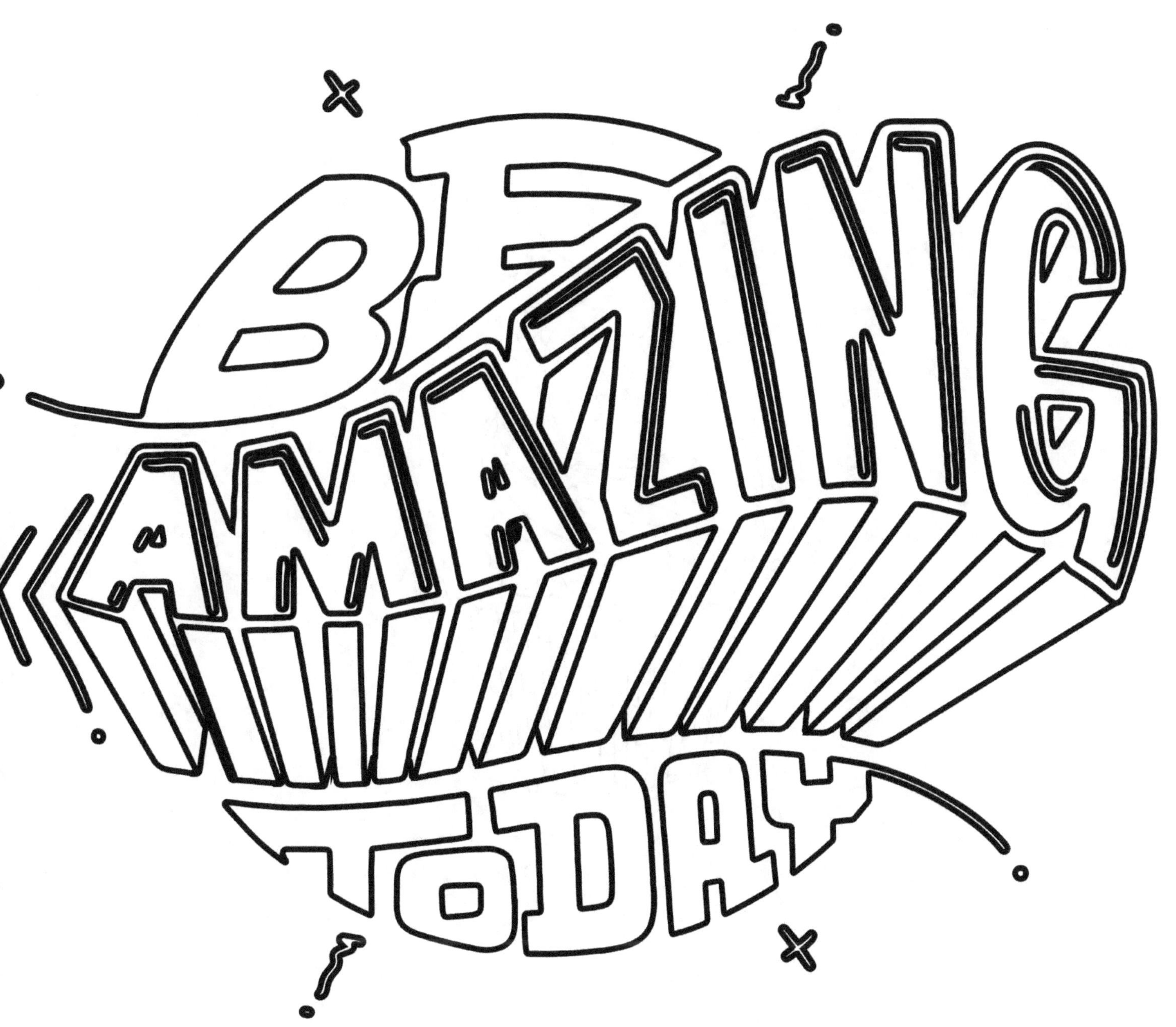

BE
AMAZING
TODAY

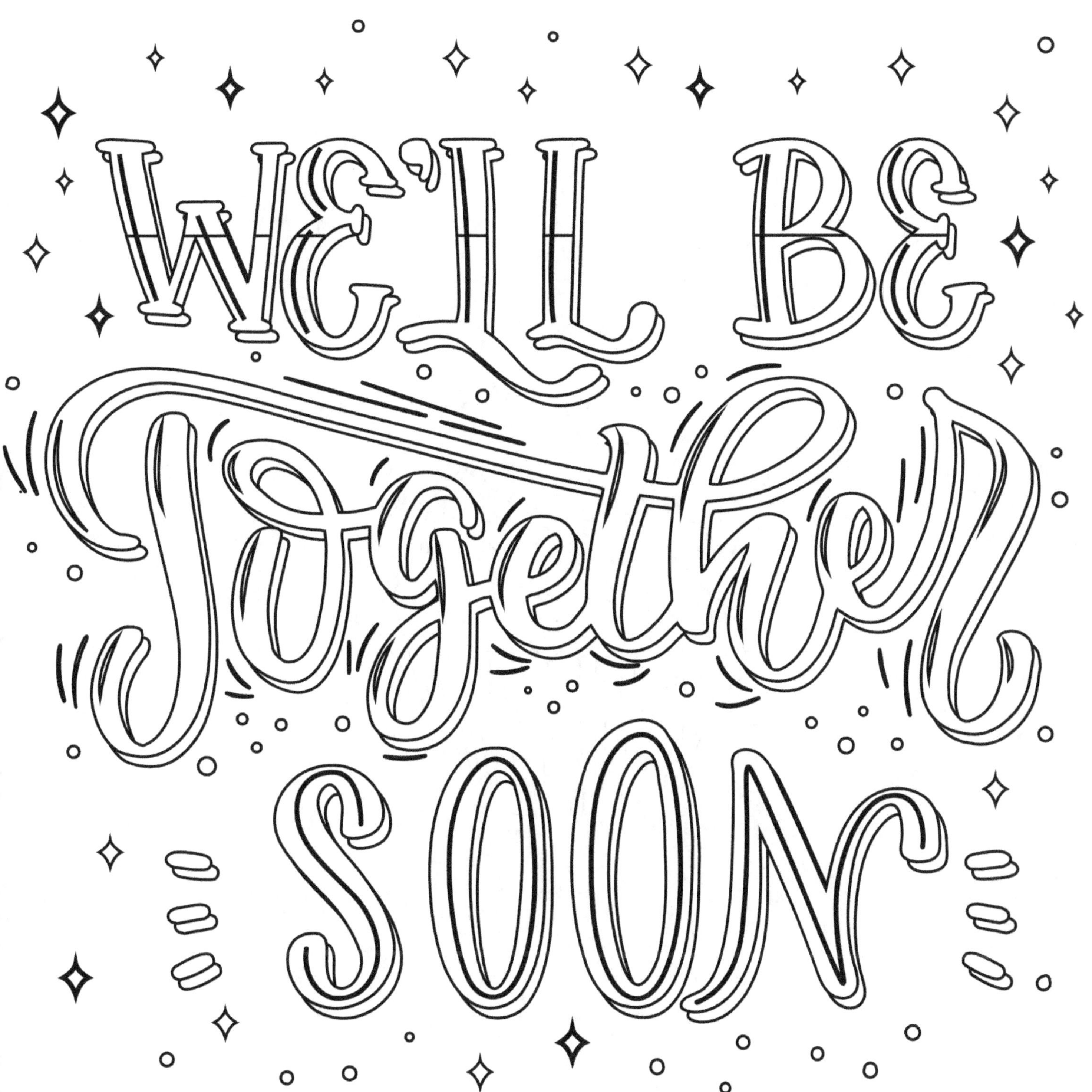

WE'LL BE
TOGETHER
SOON

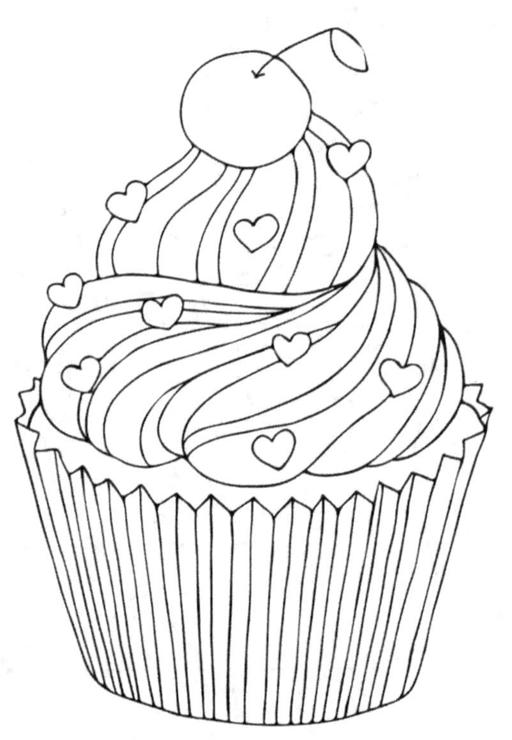

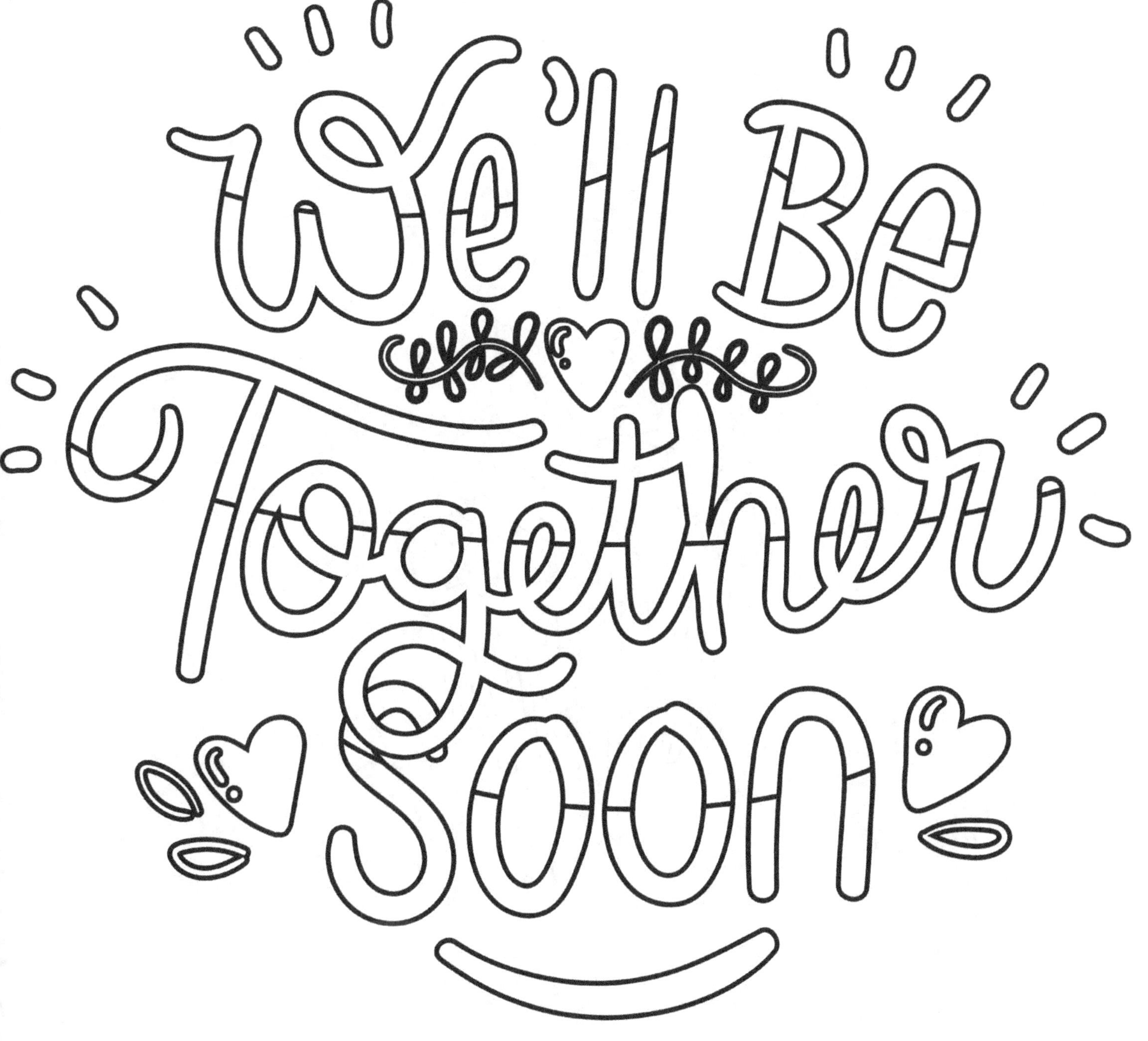

We'll Be
Together
Soon

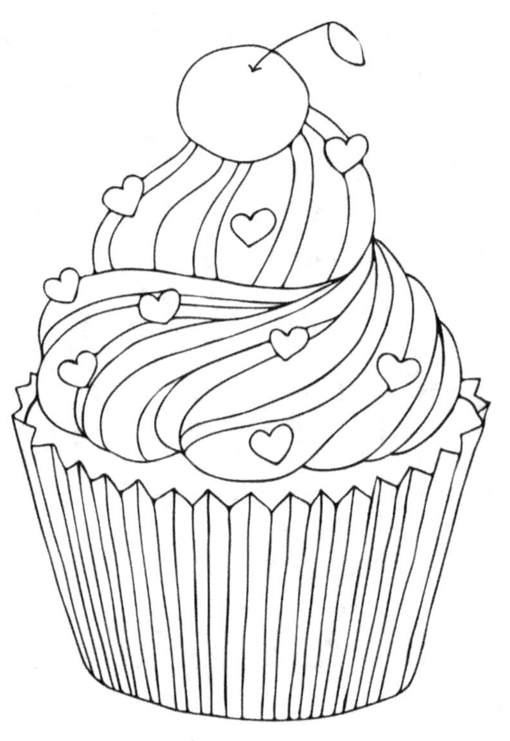

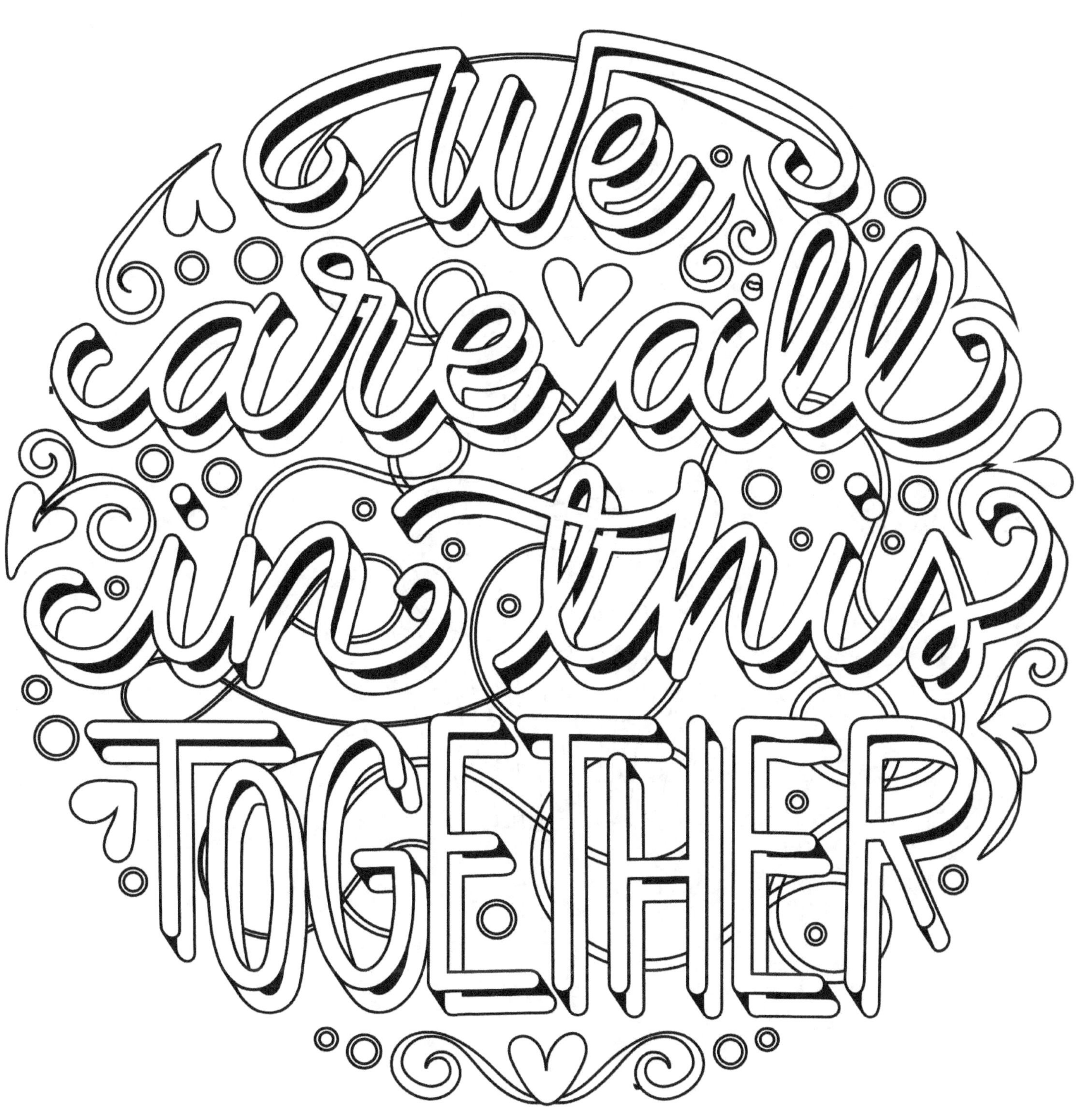
We are all in this together

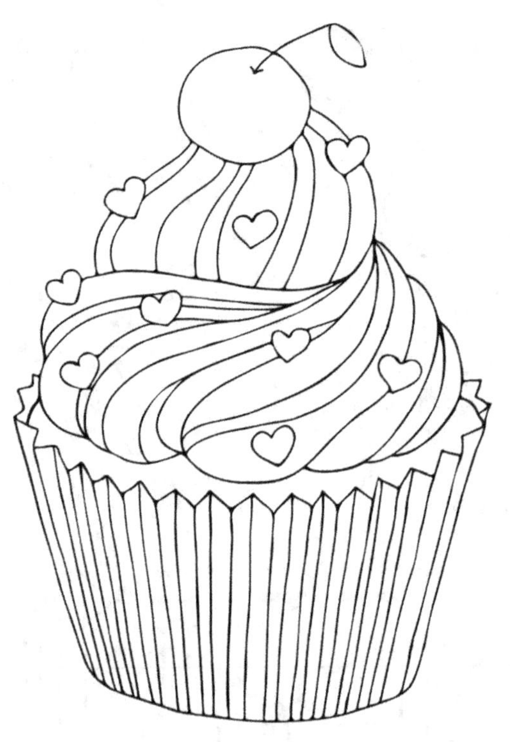

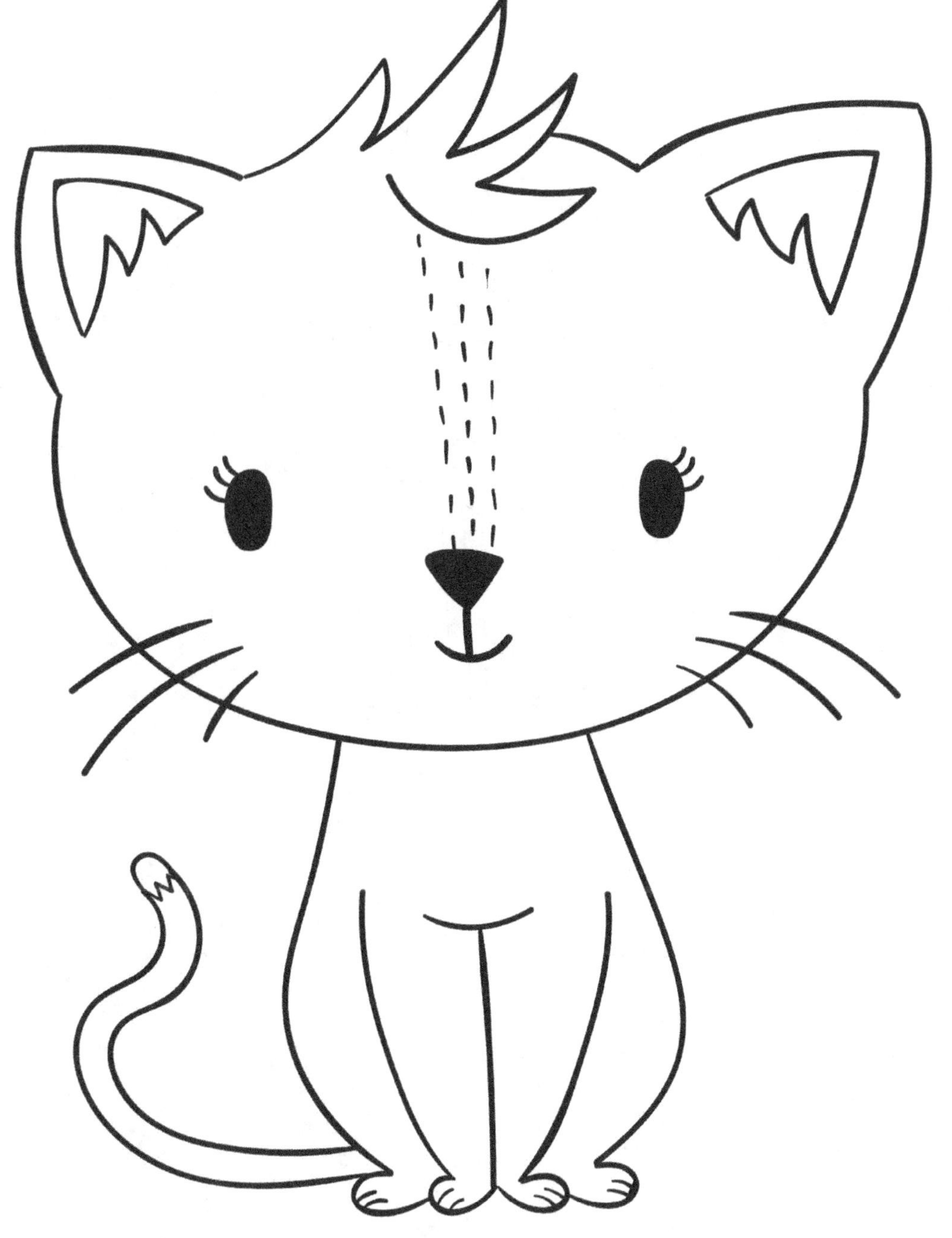

Get WELL
Soon!

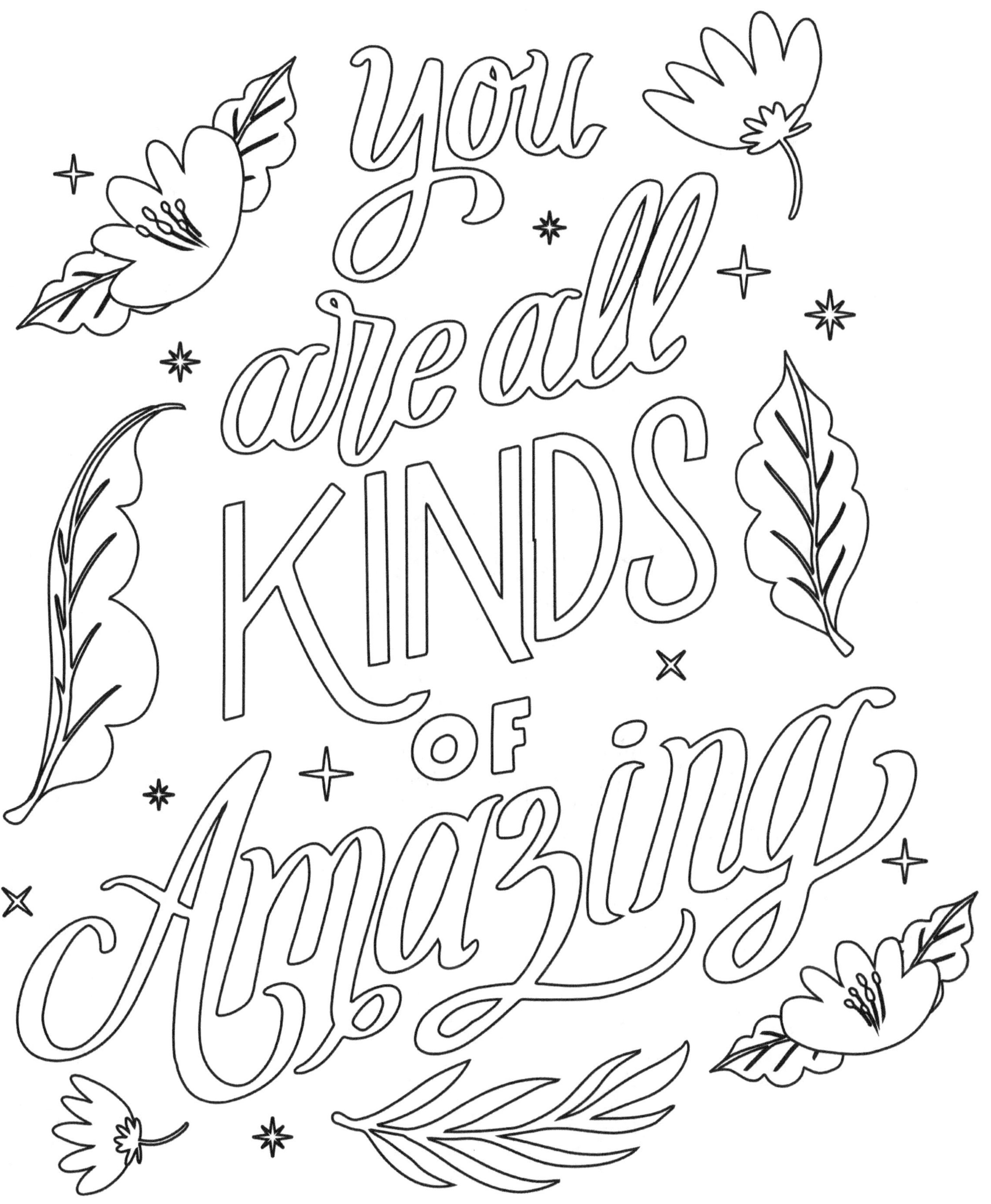

You are all KINDS OF Amazing

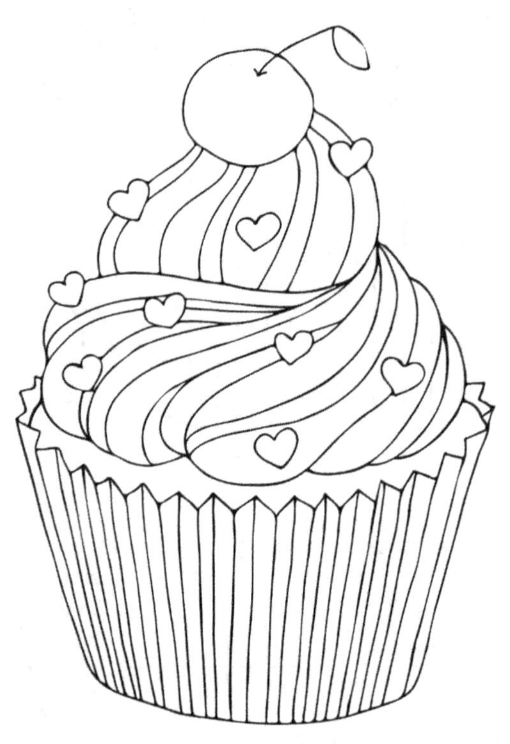

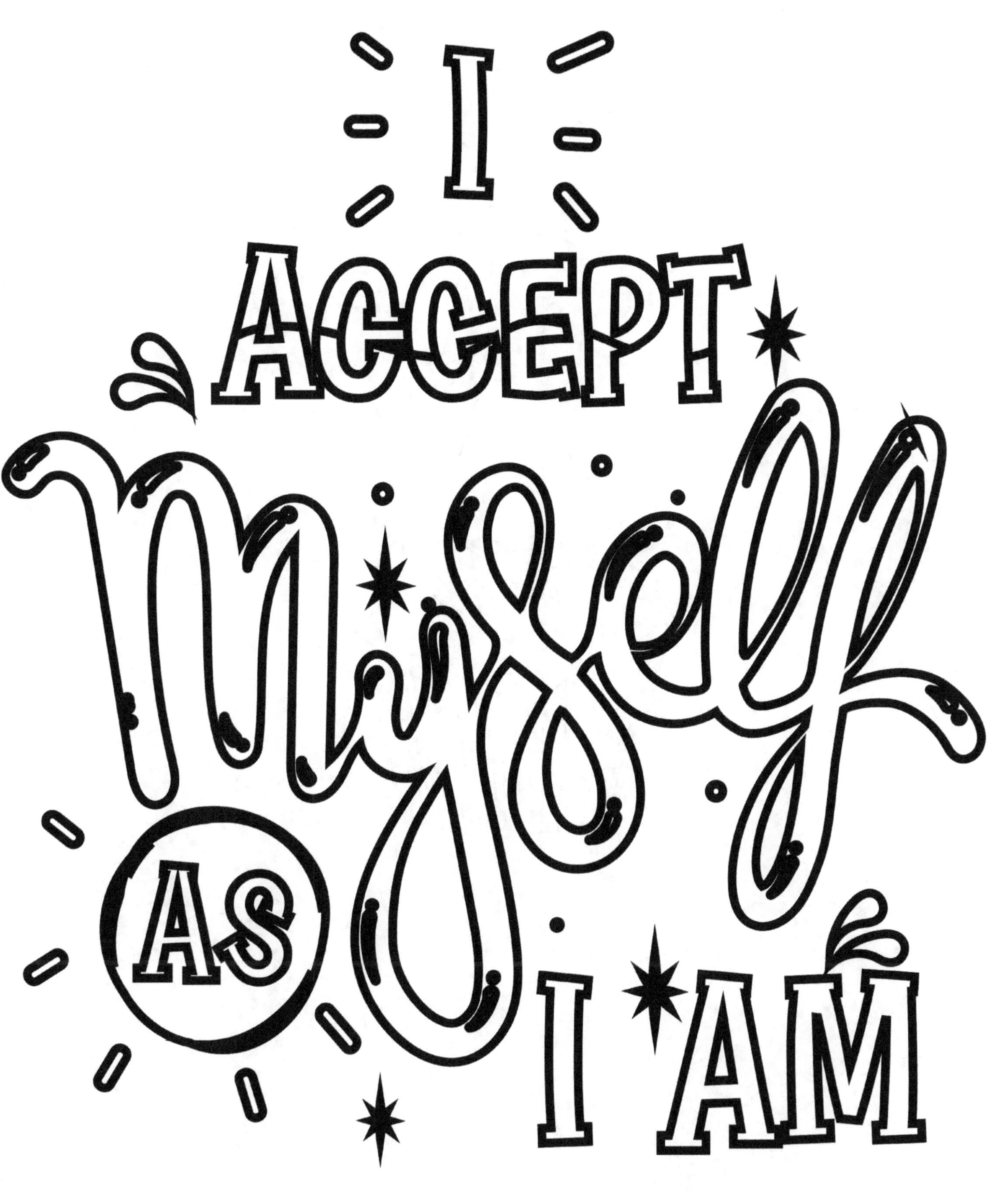

I ACCEPT MYSELF AS I AM

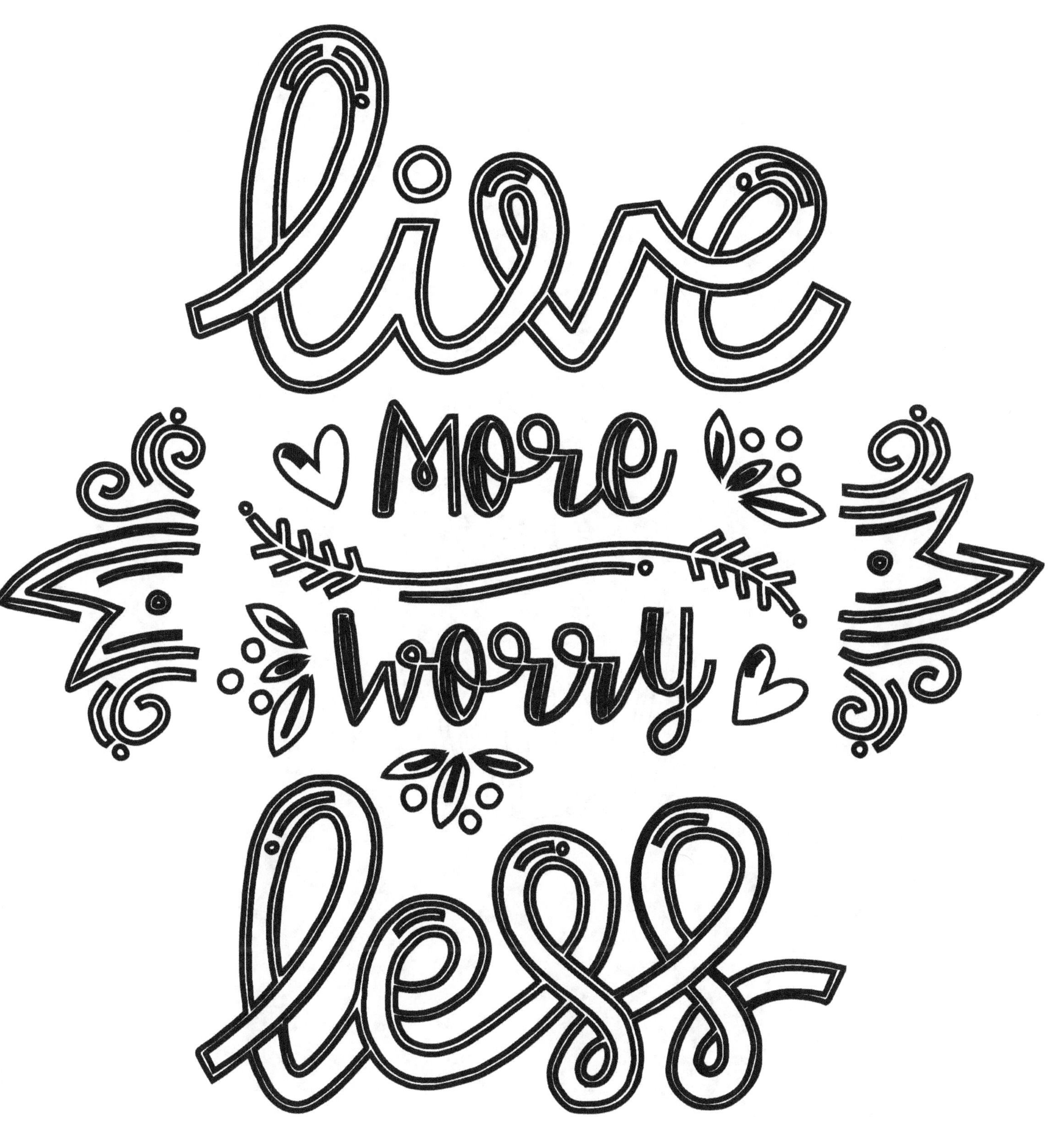

live
More
worry
less

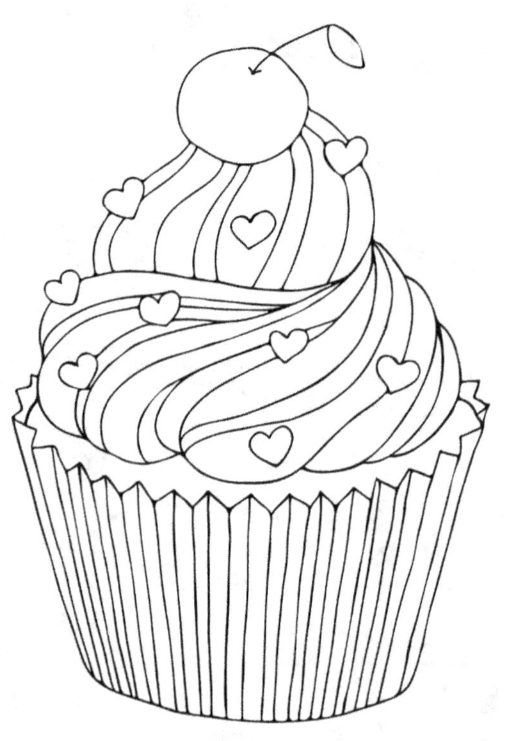

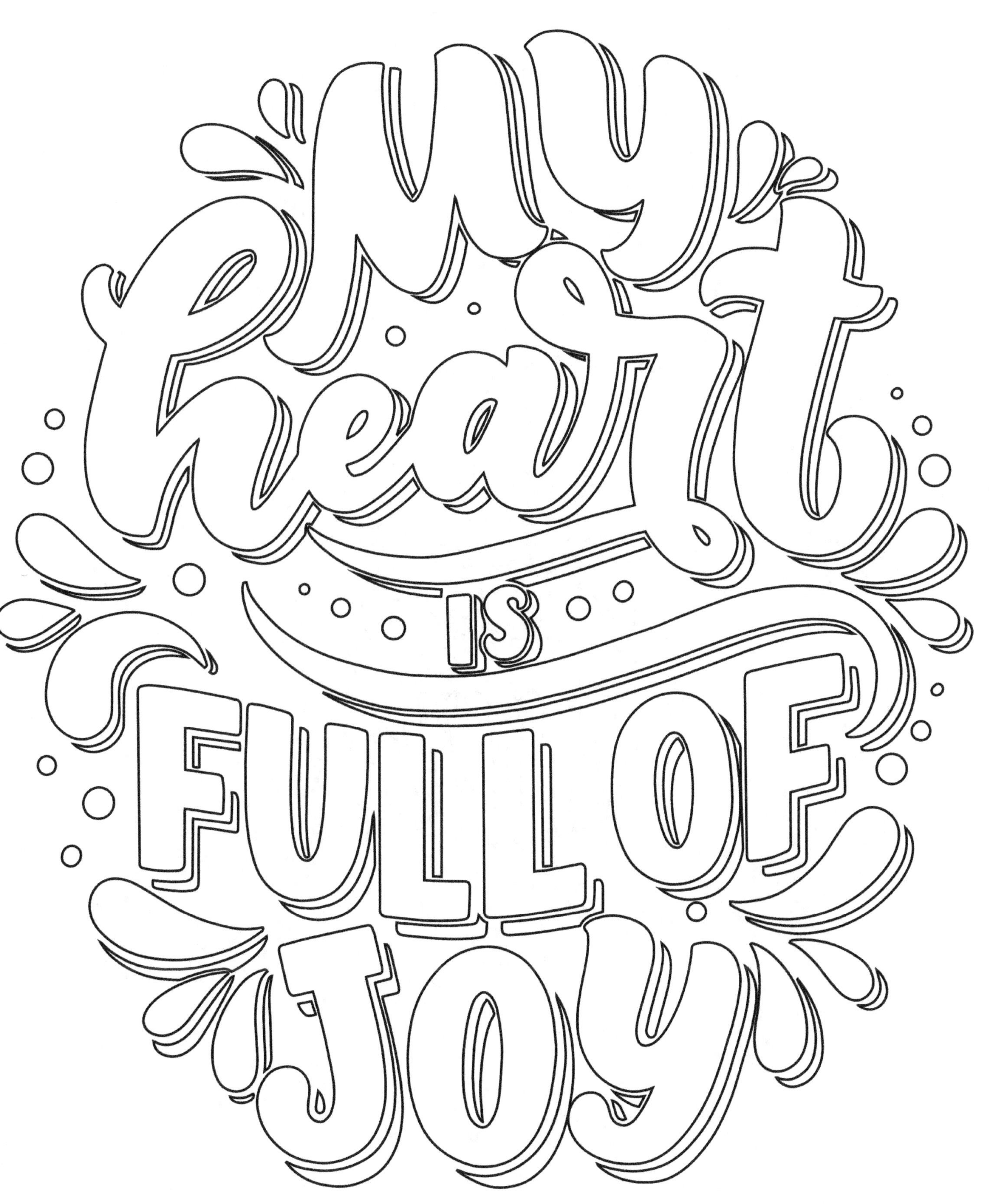
MY
HEART
IS
FULL OF
JOY

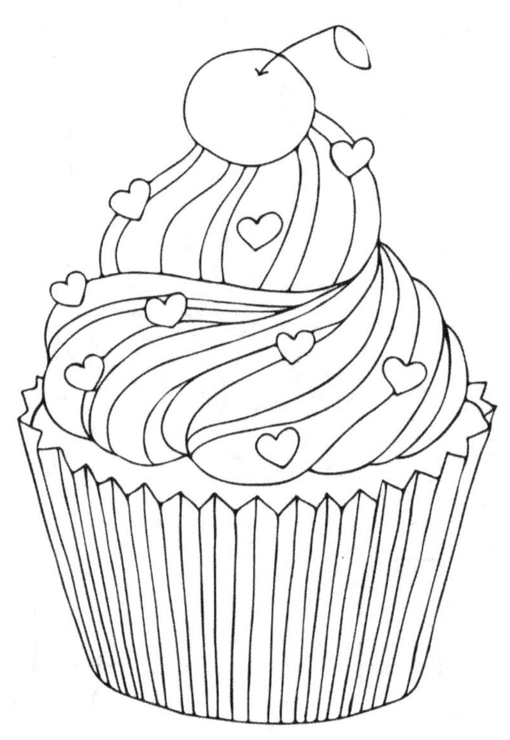

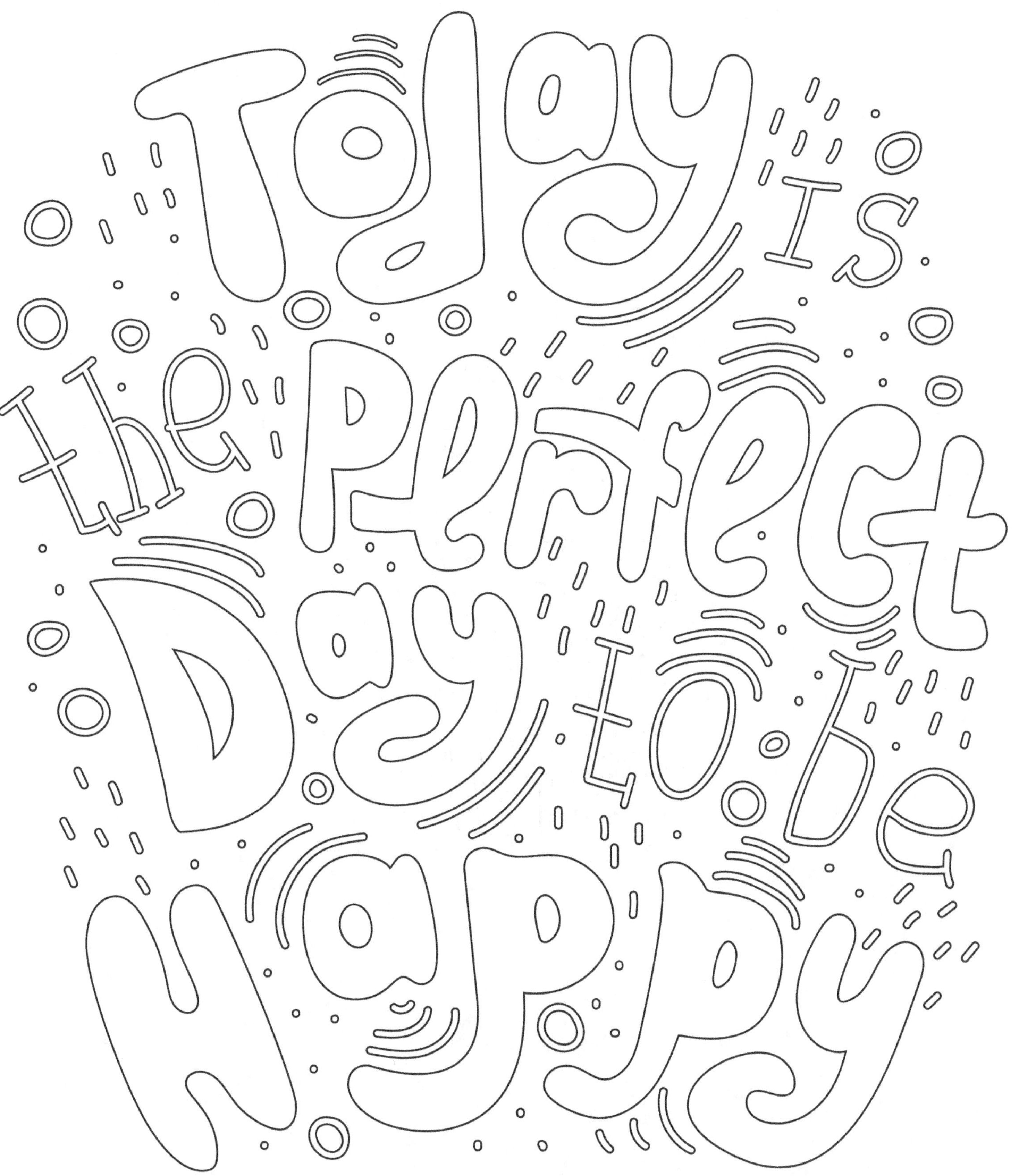

Today is the perfect day to be happy

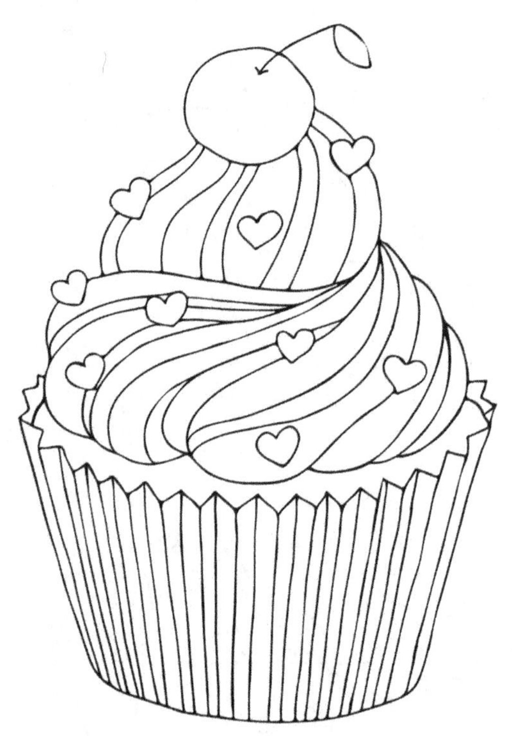

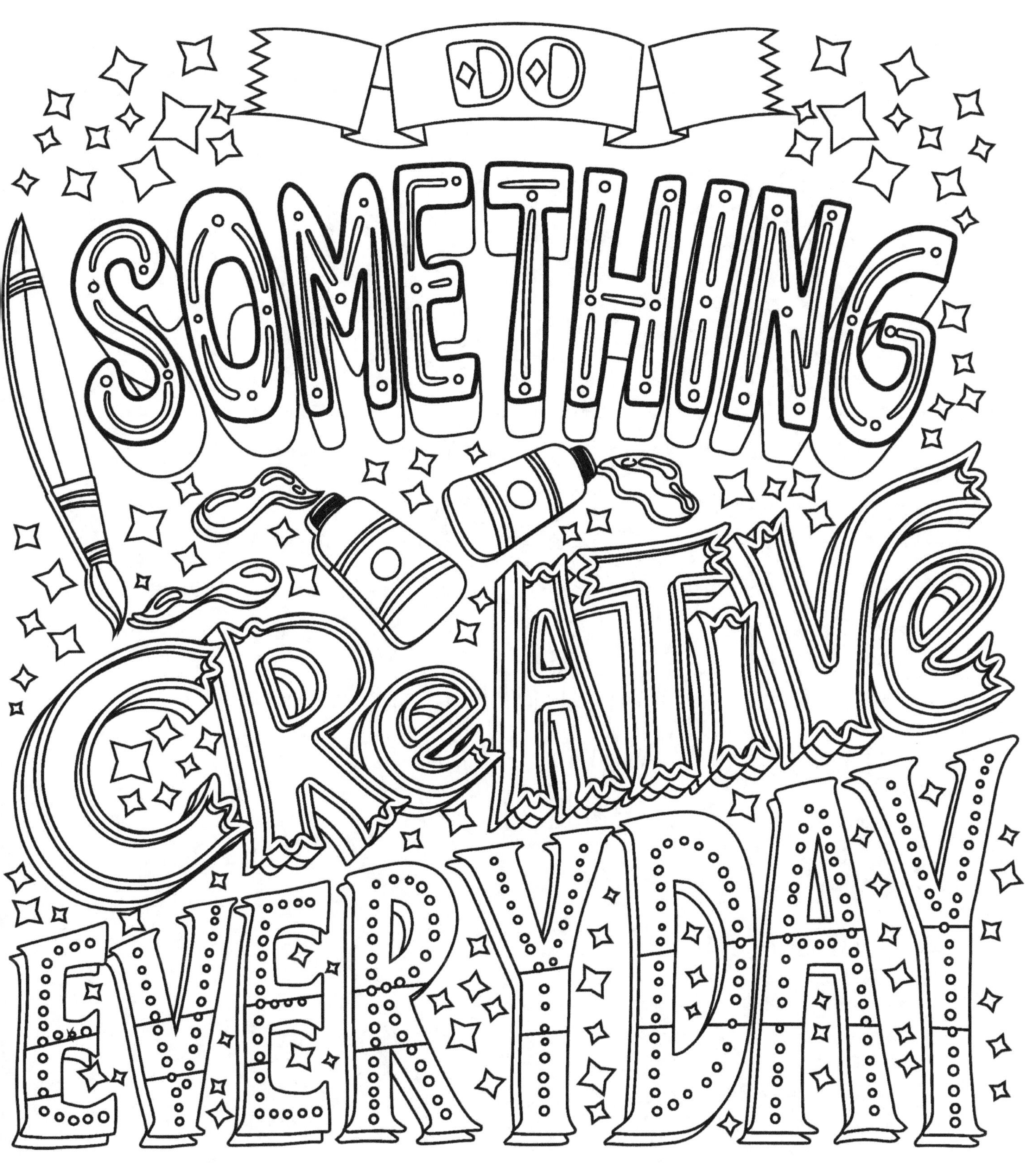
DO
SOMETHING
CREATIVE
EVERYDAY

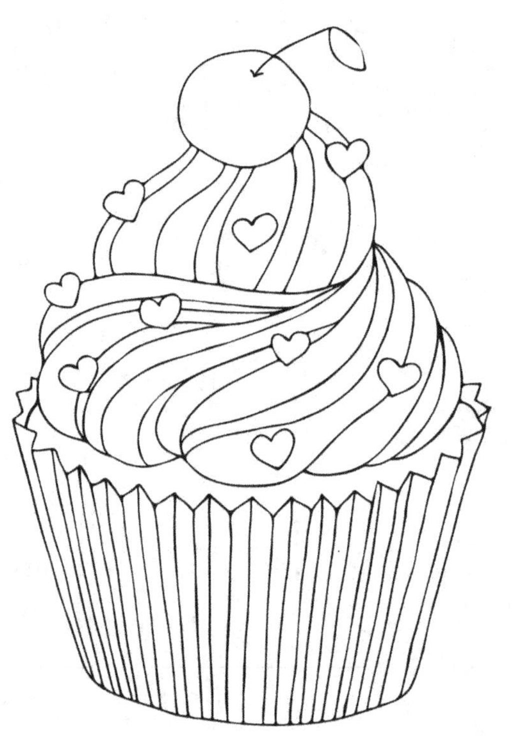

Don't
Dream
of
Winning.
Train
for it!

DO
OR
DO NOT
THERE IS
NO TRY

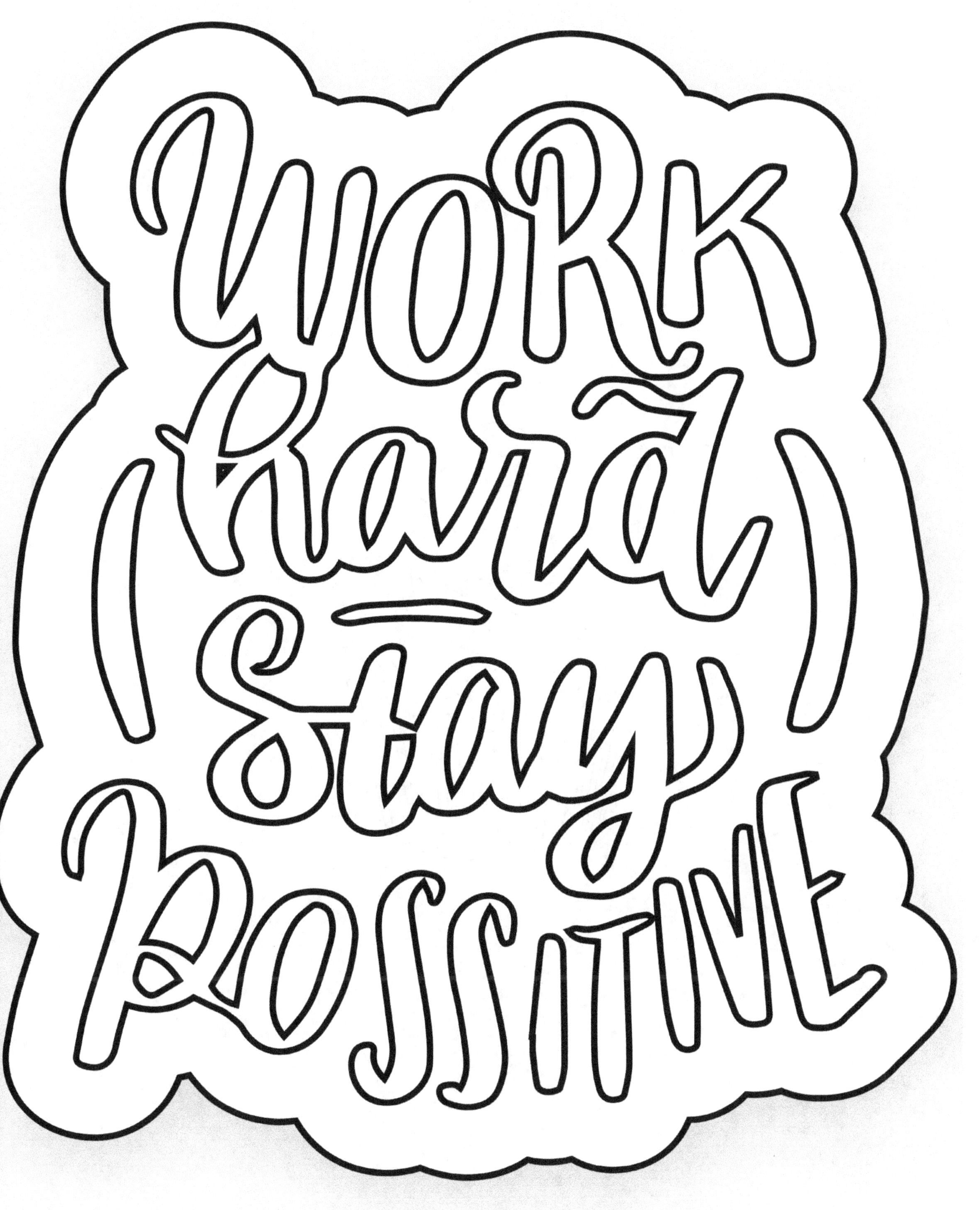
WORK
hard
stay
POSITIVE

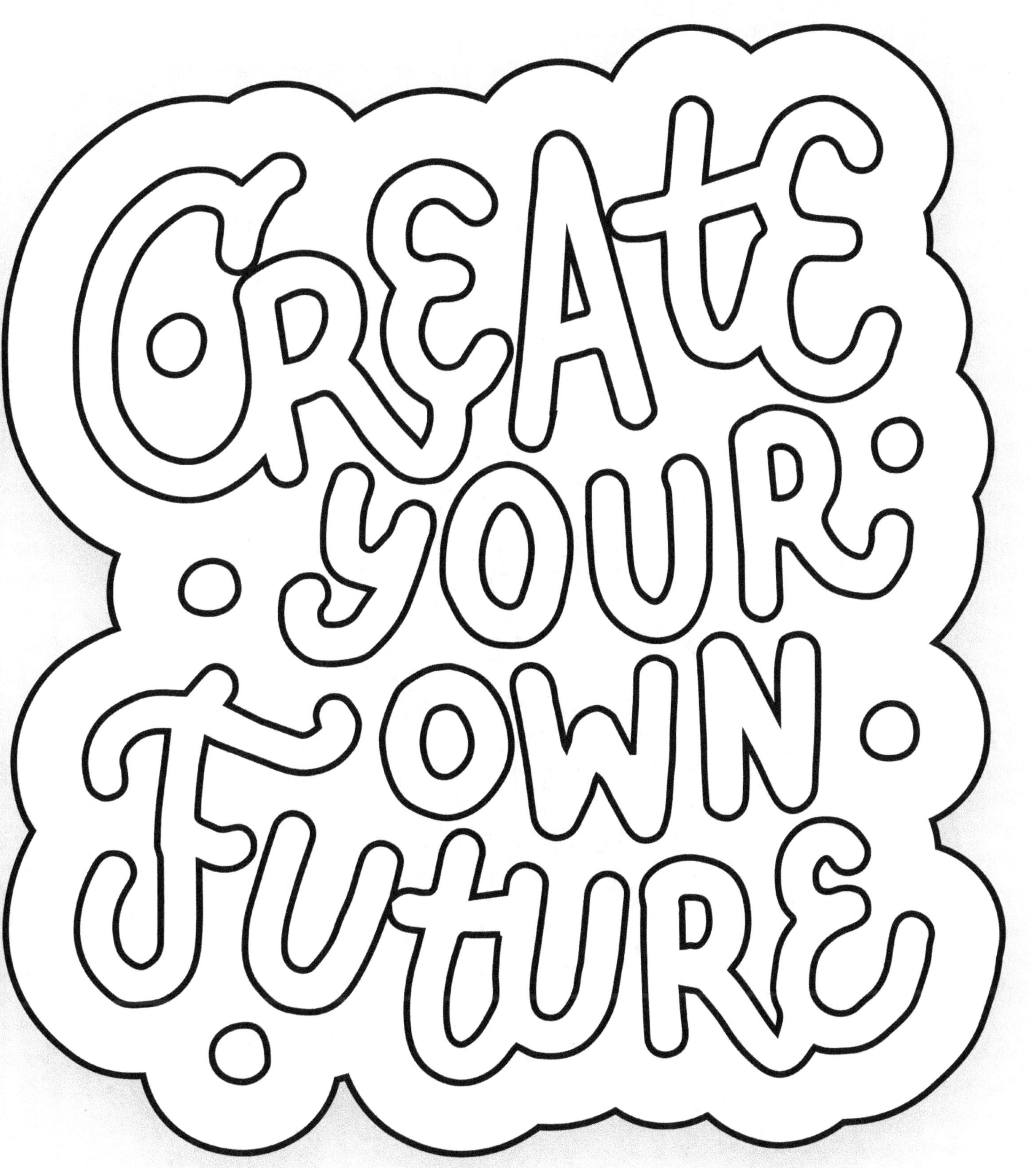

Create
your
own
Future

MAKE IT
HAPPEN
SHOCK
EVERYONE